William Jolly

Flora Macdonald in Uist

A Study of the Heroine in her Native Surroundings

William Jolly

Flora Macdonald in Uist
A Study of the Heroine in her Native Surroundings

ISBN/EAN: 9783337196301

Printed in Europe, USA, Canada, Australia, Japan

Cover: Foto ©Andreas Hilbeck / pixelio.de

More available books at **www.hansebooks.com**

FLORA MACDONALD IN UIST.

Flora Macdonald in Uist.

A Study of the Heroine

in her

Native Surroundings.

BY

WILLIAM JOLLY, F.R.S.E., F.G.S.

AUTHOR OF "JOHN DUNCAN, WEAVER AND BOTANIST," "ROBERT BURNS AT MOSSGIEL," ETC.

PERTH:
S. COWAN & CO., STRATHMORE PRINTING WORKS.

"A name that will be mentioned in history, and, if courage and fidelity are virtues, mentioned with honour."

JOHNSON.

PREFACE.

FLORA MACDONALD was at once simpler and greater than she has been pictured in popular song and story.

This outline sketch is an attempt to present her as she lived, with the requisite local colouring, and to indicate the special conditions under which so marked a personality was produced. It is a statement of the facts given as fairly as they can now be ascertained. Strangely, none of the writers on our heroine have known the Uists, a radical want in treating of one to whom they were so much. This defect has caused them to fall into errors regarding the localities and scenery, and regarding the movements of the Prince and his friends, which only local knowledge could correct; as is here partly done.

The best account yet written is her Life, by the Rev. Alexander MacGregor, late of Inverness, once minister of Kilmuir, where she is buried—a pleasantly simple, realistic, and appreciative book, though defective in style, with much original information. Her so-called "Autobiography," by her granddaughter, is a mixture of fact and fiction, full of error, and, though possessing some good things, has rightly fallen aside.

The present study is extended from papers in the *Scottish Church* of February and March last.

A perfectly critical and accurate life of Flora Macdonald, worthy of the woman and her work, remains still to be written.

POLLOKSHIELDS, *April*, 1886.

CONTENTS.

CHAP.		PAGE
I.	THE HEROINE IN HER EARLY HOME.	11
II.	THE HEROINE AT SCHOOL	22
III.	THE HEROINE AFTER CULLODEN	28
IV.	THE HEROINE IN LOOK AND SENTIMENT	37
V.	THE HEROINE'S PROTÉGÉ IN HIDING	43
VI.	THE HEROINE PREPARING FOR ACTION	52
VII.	THE HEROINE IN ACTION	61
VIII.	THE HEROINE COMPLETING HER WORK	70
IX.	THE HEROINE IN STATE CAPTIVITY	79
X.	THE HEROINE IN AFTER LIFE	86

FLORA MACDONALD IN UIST.

CHAPTER I.

THE HEROINE IN HER EARLY HOME.

WE stood by the door of a ruined cottage in the south end of South Uist, in the solitude of a tenantless waste, on a wet Sunday morning of autumn, 1879. The old man remained silent for a space contemplating the scene, and then, reverently lifting his hat in the dripping rain, as his grey locks streamed in the wind, he knelt down and kissed the worn threshold stone of the house where had been born, as he said, "a noble-hearted woman!"

The old man was our good friend, veteran in years but ever young in spirit, Professor Blackie, and the cottage was the birthplace of Flora Macdonald.

We had been sojourning together in the hospitable Uists, enjoying the unique scenery of these outlying isles; their broad, green machars or plains bordering the Atlantic, their sinuous firths, their countless lakes, their strange sandy fords across which the traveller is driven where the raging sea has flowed at last tide, their impressive treeless wildernesses, their peaked mountains, and their picturesque townships of thatched cottages, which shelter their teeming population. We had climbed the volcanic-looking crest of Hecla, the name suggestive of old Viking days, and had gazed with wonderment from that central peak, under an unclouded sky, on the unparalleled vision of the inextricable confusion of mountain and moor, sea and lake, that constitute the Long Island—visible there from the Butt of the Lewis to the hills of Barra, with Skye and the Coolins across the Minch, and the blue mainland beyond. And now, before crossing to beautiful Barra, we determined to devote our last Sunday, wet as it was, to the early home and life of that heroine, whose "name will be mentioned in history, and if courage and fidelity are virtues, mentioned with honour," as Johnson has felicitously expressed her fame, in words fitly engraved on her first tombstone.

It was a cottage having only three rooms, one on each side of the entrance, and the other opening into the kitchen on the south. Though it was thatched and unpretentious, like all others in the islands except the castles of the chiefs, it was well furnished and eminently comfortable. It stood on a green knoll facing the rising sun, in an open grassy valley. From its door, four gleaming lakes could be seen, enclosed by numerous hills, each bearing its own designation, such as Arneval, Sheval, Reneval, Askeval, and others equally euphonic, and the whole dominated on the left by the long serrated ridge of Ben More. Through the vale wanders a quiet brook, which flows into Loch Kildonan close by, with its ruined church amid its numerous graves. The burn turned a mill which gave name to the cottage itself, Airidh Mhuillin,[1] the Sheiling of the Mill, now translated into the common word, Milton, which is the present name of the large farm that includes all the land there. The old farm had attached to it the

[1] Pronounced *Ahree Voolin*, a pleasant combination of sounds, like many Gaelic words.

usual outhouses connected with agricultural life, and the dwellings of the servants; while comfortable crofters dwelt all around.

Here lived, at the beginning of last century, Ranald Macdonald, tacksman of the surrounding soil, and here, in 1722, two years after the birth of Prince Charlie, eight after the first of the Hanoverian line had ascended the throne, and in the year when fear of the elder Pretender caused Walpole to form a camp in Hyde Park, his only daughter was born. She received the beautiful name of Fionnghal,[1] the fair one, which has only an arbitrary connection with its English equivalent, the better known,

---

[1] This name is given by Bishop Forbes, the author of "The Lyon in Mourning," an invaluable account of the Rebellion, as "Funnivella," Flora being called by him "Miss Funnivella."

Flora. She was well connected, for her father was not distantly related to his chief, Clanranald, and her mother, Marion, was the daughter of the minister of the parish, the Rev. Angus Macdonald, known as "the strong minister," from his immense strength, who had married into the family of an Argyllshire laird in Kintyre.

Flora's father died when she was but two years old, and her mother was abducted to Sleat in Skye, when her child was but six, by Hugh Macdonald of Armadale, who became her husband. Little Flora showed, even at that early age, some traits of character that afterwards made her famous, by choosing to remain with her brother Angus in the island of her birth, rather than go to the Isle of Mist, where her mother had a happy home. She thus came to be brought up greatly as an orphan, under the kindly care of her only surviving brother, in that secluded hollow.

Though sequestered, it was a very pleasant place in which to spend a childhood, the very spot where Wordsworth might have placed his Lucy, to be influenced

> "With high objects, with enduring things,
> With life and nature; purifying thus
> The elements of feeling and of thought."

There were close at hand the quiet pastoral valley, the companion brook, the big lake that received its waters, the strange wheel it moved, the fascinating dusty mill, the varied life of the farm, the old church and its tombstones, with the surrounding wonderful hills, all enjoyed by the contemplative child. Then, not far off, were the rolling dunes by the Atlantic, on whose green, thymy slopes she played, and the great ocean itself, heaving in mightiest billows or reposing in impressive calm; with the weird-looking islands of St. Kilda and her sister rocks, out on the far horizon, sometimes seen with wonderful distinctness. By the shore, she was often seen to watch and wander all alone, in a way the folk deemed strange. At night, she could listen to the thunder of the waves as she lay in her cosy bed in her cottage home.

She thus grew up unusually thoughtful and self-contained, and though relishing much the games of childhood, she was greatly satisfied with the joy of her own communings. The life she led, without brothers or sisters, in the society of older people, made such a child act and speak more sagely than her years. The powerful character, also, of the uncommon scenes amidst which she was thus reared, no doubt contributed to the rare self-possession and calm independence that characterised her from early days.

She was, nevertheless, bright and cheerful in company, and was much taken out by friends throughout the island. A favourite everywhere, she was not less so with the grand folks at Nunton, the mansion of Clanranald, away north in Benbecula, where she was a frequent visitor. She also visited much among the numerous crofters then scattered over South Uist. These had comfortable holdings on the plains, and hill pasture for cattle and sheep in the mountains, to which many of them removed in summer. They were intelligent and shrewd, with a natural culture in speech and manner unknown in the Lowlands; and they lived in happy relations with the tacksmen, such as Angus Macdonald, and with their paternal chiefs. They dwelt in "townships," and conducted their affairs through an admirable joint organization, with independence and success. They were well versed in the abundant literature of legend, poetry, and proverb, which are still preserved in the memories of the inhabitants of these distant islands more than elsewhere in the Highlands.

Happy intercourse with these good folks, in those days before evictions had paralysed them, was an important element in Flora's training, and attached her to the land and the people with undying affection.[1] She became proficient in the attractive folk-lore

---

[1] For details of the old township life of the Uists, see the excellent paper in Appendix A. to the Report of the recent *Crofter Commission*, by Mr. Alex. A. Carmichael, whose knowledge of these islands, and of Flora Macdonald, is unrivalled, and to whom I am indebted for much information.

she heard so much repeated and sung in the cottages round. She could feelingly recite ancient Ossianic lays, and fervently sing the old Celtic songs to the sweet old tunes. She thus became in many ways precocious, and grew up a wise little maiden, informed beyond her years.

CHAPTER II.

THE HEROINE AT SCHOOL

FLORA'S formal education was by no means neglected, for she attended school in the neighbourhood and made uncommon progress. When she reached the age of thirteen, Lady Clanranald, who loved her as a daughter, practically adopted the solitary child into her family, where, for three years, along with her own daughters, she enjoyed the tuition of a governess. By this means, Flora's accomplishments were increased, and she became an expert player on the spinet, on which she produced Gaelic airs with all the variations and spirit of the pipes. She endeared herself to every one, but especially to Clanranald and his wife, who became her closest friends for life.

To her brother Angus, who cultivated the ancestral farm, and was noted equally for his strength and goodness, she was greatly attached, for he had been to her the kindest of foster fathers. Though she had seen comparatively little of her mother since her removal to Skye, she had a real affection for her, and crossed the Minch at intervals to visit her.

In Skye, Flora won the high regard of the beautiful Lady Margaret Macdonald, one of the handsome Montgomeries of Eglinton Castle, and the wife of Sir Alexander Macdonald of the Isles, who then lived at Monkstadt in the north end of the island. When seventeen, Flora was for eight months a cherished member of their circle. She also became intimate with the family of the good, genial factor, Macdonald of Kingsburgh, a connection that more than any other shaped her after life.

After visits to Uist to nurse her sick brother and see her friends at Nunton, Flora was sent by Lady Margaret to Edinburgh, to complete her education. She was placed in a high-class school, situated in a close off the then fashionable High Street. She always stayed, however, with Lord Macdonald's family, when, like others of rank and riches then, they visited the metropolis during winter. She studied hard, and became generally accomplished. In music, in particular, she surpassed most ladies of her time.

She mingled in the best society that yearly assembled to the gaieties of the Northern Athens of that day, and twice visited the

Countess of Eglinton in Ayrshire, who, with her seven daughters, then ruled the fashionable Scottish world. In the drawing-room, Flora was the centre of many a group, charmed with her unobtrusive sweetness, and attracted by her rare Highland melodies, which were delightfully rendered by voice and spinet. Everywhere she won golden opinions, by her bright intelligence, amiable disposition, and gentle and polite manners.

She remained in Edinburgh more than three pleasant years, and then returned to Skye in Sir Alexander's party, a rarely cultivated woman of twenty-three.

But Flora could not long be absent from Uist, and to its mountains and quiet machars she speedily returned, in June, 1745. Uist was not only her birthplace, but her home. There she had spent all her early years, except when she went to Skye and Edinburgh.

To it she returned after her adventures with the Prince, and again after her imprisonment in London. There she chiefly lived until her marriage; and at Milton, she dwelt for two years after her return from America.

Bare, treeless, unattractive, and drenched in water both by earth and sky, as it looks to most strangers, Uist possesses uncommon beauties to all who have seen its unique scenery. To Flora, it was the dearest, fairest land on earth; as it is, with unusual fervour, to all its sons and daughters. She could ardently echo its praises as sung by Mac-Codrum, the poet of these islands, who flourished in her day, and who now lies under a self-selected block of gneiss in the graveyard of Kilmuir, on its lone eminence, in North Uist—

"A land that faces the ocean wild,
But with summer sweetness mellow and mild.

Green knolls with yellow sheaves are there,
And snow is shy, and frost is rare;
With smiling machars by the sea,
Where marigolds and daisies be.
A land in all right fair to view,
With well-girt lads of healthy hue."[1]

[1] Translated by Professor Blackie in his delightful *Language and Literature of the Highlands*, which reveals little known riches in Gaelic poetry.

CHAPTER III.

THE HEROINE AFTER CULLODEN.

BENBECULA is a low, flat island lying between North and South Uist, from which it is separated by two strange fords, the north ford being three miles wide and dangerous, and the south about one mile, over which the Atlantic tides roll twice a day, but across which you can drive at the ebb! The island is named from the solitary eminence it contains, and from these two fords—the island of the Ben between the fords. From the top of this low hill, locally dignified as Ben Eval, a most extraordinary scene presents itself; of the whole sinuous island, especially of its eastern shores, an untenanted, desert wild, of moss, moor, lake and sea, which terminates in the point of Rossnish, a name compounded of both Gaelic and Norse, both syllables meaning the same thing, a cape.

The western side of the island, however, being part of the flat machars of the Uists, is cultivated into smiling fields and pastures, and it is there that the people mainly dwell. In their midst, on the site of an old nunnery, not far from an old castle of the Clanranalds, still stands the mansion of Nunton, yet hospitably inhabited. In Nunton, the Clanranalds held high state when the Prince was in hiding, as lords of all these lands, though now their descendants possess not one rood of their old domains. Thither the family had removed in the Fifteen, when Allan the chief was slain at Sheriffmuir, and when the grander house of Ormiclade in South Uist was burnt down, to remain ever since a staring ruin.[1] In Nunton, Clanranald lived when he and his brave lady risked liberty, life and all, for Prince Charlie. There Flora found the happiest of homes at that romantic period; and there she took chief part in the kindly councils for his rescue. There also Clanranald's descendants dwelt till the islands were purchased by the lowland millionaire, Colonel Gordon of Cluny.

When Flora left Edinburgh for the Hebrides, the whole social world was volcanic with rumours and machinations connected with the exiled Stuarts. A month after her return to Milton, Prince Charlie

---

[1] Strangely, all former writers have located the Clanranalds in Ormiclade, at the Rebellion, an error which has vitiated the correct explanation of the movements of the Prince and his friends in Uist.

landed a few miles distant, at populous Eriska, on the 23rd of July, 1745. This was the first British soil he touched, a small island off the south end of Uist, where he scattered the seeds of a convolvulus, now flourishing on the spot and known as "the Prince's flower."

Then followed, in startling succession, the short but brilliant acts in the foolhardy drama of this last war in Britain—the lifting of the red standard at Glenfinnan on August 19th, the enthusiastic gathering of the clans, the bright entry into Edinburgh, the dashing victory at Prestonpans, the unparalleled march into the heart of England, the orderly and successful retreat, and the dire overthrow on blood-stained Drummossie, on 16th April, 1746.

During these stirring events, Flora had chiefly resided with her hospitable friends at

Nunton, in Benbecula. Her bright society and sound judgment had done much to cheer them in those troublous times. Clanranald and his lady, though warmly sympathising with the Prince, had wisely refused to join his mad adventure. Their eldest son, notwithstanding, had done so from the first, and his rebellion had distressed them greatly, as not only endangering himself but compromising the whole family.

Nine days after Culloden, the Clanranald circle was startled into painful insecurity by the news that the Prince himself had landed in Benbecula, from Moidart on the mainland! With incredible speed, for his footsteps were dogged, royalist redcoats arrived in increasing numbers, and scattered themselves all over the islands, occupying every ford and searching every suspected corner, under keen and unscrupulous officers. Each hour increased the danger to the unfortunate fugitive, with thirty thousand set on his devoted head.

What was to be done? Clanranald and his lady were truly loyal to the Government. Even had it been otherwise, the slightest assistance to the outlaw involved certain ruin, if not death. Yet, though filled with natural alarm at the risk they ran, they acted with generous humanity and admirable courage. They determined to befriend the Prince, and, if possible, accomplish his escape. A secret council was held, at which Flora took active part, and it was deemed best to forward Charles by boat to Stornoway, from which, as a seaport, it was thought there was a better chance of reaching France. With a brave, selected crew, under the charge of one of Clanranald's trusty followers, the bold Donald Macleod, the Prince set out on his perilous voyage northwards, on the 29th of April, two days after he had landed at Benbecula.

On the 12th of May, the good Clanranalds, agitated between extreme hopes and fears as to the success of their plan, were thrown into new consternation by the entrance of the faithful Donald at daybreak, to announce the return of the unlucky Prince to the same spot, after increasing jeopardy! The tearful gathering was cheered by the bright confidence of Flora. Her courage and hopefulness had proved a solace all through their trials—as abundantly acknowledged by them—and they now greatly restored her friends to calmness.

Clanranald, in the guise of a huntsman, at once set out for the Prince's hiding-place. It was a wretched hut some miles distant, not far from Rossnish, the bleak easterly point of the island just described. There his crew had been compelled to cook the very shellfish on the shore for food. Next morning, full supplies were sent from the mansion by the famous Neil MacEachan, an intelligent young tutor in Clanranald's family. Neil had been intended for the priesthood, but never took orders, being for a time schoolmaster of South Uist, where the Rev. John Macaulay, grandfather of Lord Macaulay, was then minister. He had spent some years in Paris, and could converse with the Prince in French. In time, he became the father of Marshal Macdonald, who was ennobled by the great Napoleon as Duke of Tarentum.

A safer retreat became daily more necessary. One was at length selected in the wild mountain range that skirts the east side of South Uist, where the approach of an enemy was difficult, and where his friends could more easily communicate with him. This was in Glen Corrodale, on the eastern front of Hecla, close by the sea. There, in the most secluded valley in the island, Prince Charles remained in perfect security for several weeks, till successfully conducted by our heroine right through the fiery circle that hourly closed nearer upon him.

The Uists were soon reduced to a state of military siege. Not a house was sacred from constant intrusion. No one could pass from place to place, or converse with a neighbour, without rude questioning as to his goings and doings. Every hour increased the vigilance of the enemy, so that, as Flora expressed it, "not even a sparrow could escape without their knowledge and consent."

CHAPTER IV.

THE HEROINE IN LOOK AND SENTIMENT.

BUT how looked Flora Macdonald when thus bursting into fame? What was the appearance at this time of our "pretty young rebel," as she was called by General Campbell, who afterwards apprehended her? Certainly not like the stage heroine of general expectation or popular song; but something far simpler and better.

A portrait lies before me, taken from a painting by an artist, Robertson, when she was in London, which bears the stamp of truth, in its genuine simplicity, and which has been fitly engraved as our frontispiece. It presents as unaffected a girl as one could desire to see, with modest, open look, large, clear eyes, sweet, strong mouth, high, kindly forehead and broad, thoughtful brow. One white rose crowns her simple hair, and her dress is plain tartan, with a plaid hung on the left shoulder; without ornament, except a long necklace of beads, probably one of her many rich gifts, hung round her neck and attached to a knot of ribbon on her open breast. There is truly pictured the quiet maiden who did so calmly and unaffectedly the greatest deed of her day.

She is thus described, in blunt and graphic terms, by Bishop Forbes, the author of the "Lyon in Mourning," who met her frequently in Leith Roads on her way to London. "She was," he says, "of low stature, of a fair complexion, and well enough shaped. Her behaviour in company was so easy, modest, and well adjusted, that every visitant was much surprised;" more so, no doubt, than we who now know her training, for they thought her merely a Highland maiden from the western moors.' "Although she was easy and cheerful," he continues, " yet she had a certain mixture of gravity in all her behaviour which became her situation exceedingly well, and set her off to great advantage. One could not discern by her conversation," he says in astonishment, " that she had spent," as he wrongly thought, " all her former days in the Highlands."

The sentiments of our heroine in undertaking the daring and dangerous rescue of Charles Edward are noteworthy. She was then as firmly loyal to the reigning house as she was when her husband and children afterwards fought and suffered for it in America.

The fact that she was not a Jacobite adds brighter lustre to her conduct: for, as Professor Blackie observed in regard to it, "it is not so easy to be heroic on the cool water of human brotherhood as on the hot wine of political enthusiasm."

Her determination was little moved by the exciting romance of the position; though she had no lack of the poetic fervour inherent in Celtic blood. If one trait more than another characterised Flora Macdonald throughout life, it was the practical absence of romantic imagination, and the possession of an equable temperament, good sense, and firm judgment, which even the worship and flattery of a nation and the adulations of rank could not unbalance or excite to vanity. She appears to have been swayed purely by humanity for deep distress, by natural pity for a brave and unfortunate man, surrounded by implacable foes seeking his destruction. This womanly commiseration, uniting with uncommon firmness of purpose, prudent capacity for execution, calm courage, and a real Joan-of-Arc faith in Heaven's protection in such an enterprise, resulted in the chivalrous heroism that has made her name immortal. As she afterwards said to Prince Frederick, father of George Third, when he expressed surprise at her "daring rebellion," she would have done the same for him had she found him in like need.

The idea that she was in love with the Prince, as uttered in popular song, is absolutely groundless, and deserves not a moment's notice. Had it been true, her devotion would still have been remarkable, but poor and small compared with the reality.

Flora's greatest anxiety in attempting his deliverance was the real danger or worse evil in which she might involve her friends, especially the family of her chief. This fear she often expressed to them, a further proof of her kindly thoughtfulness, and of the absence of the self-absorbed glamour which the enterprise might reasonably have roused, and which might well have overborne one so young and inexperienced. From this care, she was greatly relieved by the quiet courage of Lord and especially Lady Clanranald, who, while rightly doing all they could to protect themselves, urged and helped her in every way to undertake the peril.

CHAPTER V.

THE HEROINE'S PROTÉGÉ IN HIDING.

SEVERAL years ago, some good friends accompanied me from the manse of South Uist on the green machars by the Atlantic, across the mountains, to Glen Corrodale, on the eastern shore. We ascended through the narrow pass that separates Hecla from Ben More, by "St. Columba's Seat," where the saint is said to have addressed the heathen; past the lonely tarn in Glen Hillisdale, under the black, precipitous front of the Ben, its top hidden in cloud; through scenery wild, bare, and grand, the only living sound being the croaking of a raven and his mate. Crossing the shoulder of the valley close by the Minch, we dropped into the Glen, which, green and pastoral, runs rapidly upwards to the steep rocks of Hecla. No sign of human habitation appeared, except the ruins of a single hut, and the scene, though pleasant, was intensely lonely.

We climbed to the cottage, and behind it found the cave where Prince Charlie had hidden during the most perilous period of his wanderings. It is situated high up on the north side of the valley not far from the shore, and shows no external marks of its existence. It commands an uninterrupted sweep of both sea and land. At its mouth, the distant peaks of Mull are clearly visible. From the ridge above, the broad Minch stretches full in view, with Rum and Eigg and the dim Mainland; and to the right, rise the western fronts of Hecla and Ben More. Every sail that passes can be seen with ease, an all-important point to a fugitive, for whose capture the sea was hourly dotted with craft, bearing fell foes; while a scout on the rocks above could at once detect every unaccustomed sight and sound. The only approach from the western side, where the soldiers were, was by the wild path we had traversed, or by the rugged shore round the north end of Hecla. Both of these the eager but fearful redcoats seem to have mostly shunned.

The cave consists of a natural hollow, the result of decay in a black basaltic dike which traverses the Fundamental Gneiss of the hill. It is ten feet square and about four feet high, and is scooped out of the base of a cliff which faces the south. The bottom is wet with moisture dripping through the rock, but the place could easily be made comfortable. It would appear to have been protected during the Prince's abode by a kind of ante-chamber roofed with heather. Another cave, which we visited, on the banks of the stream below, still more hidden from sight, could give excellent shelter in sudden need; and this extremity several times occurred.

The narrow and mountainous eastern shores of Uist were then inhabited by many thriving crofters, who lived by cultivating the ground, fishing the neighbouring seas and rearing sheep on the hills. Glen Corrodale itself, however, was inhabited by only two families, being reserved as a sheep run, on account of its good pasture, by the crofters who then dwelt on the coast in the next valley to the north. The fact that, in his seclusion, he was thus surrounded on all sides by the people, who knew the cave well, was doubtless a source of greater safety than even the bogs of Benbecula. It also explains the possibility of messengers and visitors reaching him without the suspicion that would have been roused had he hidden in a less frequented spot. No better retreat for the Outlaw could therefore have been selected; for it was wisely chosen by friends who knew every corrie, rock and lochan in these tortuous islands.[1]

Since then, however, these eastern shores have all been depopulated and are now a tenantless waste, without a single habitation except the huts of shepherds tending their flocks on the hills. The present ruined cottage in the Glen was erected for one of these,

[1] These facts regarding the former population of the eastern shores, I have received, with corroboration, from Mr. Carmichael.

and the herd that accompanied our party had occupied it for ten years, using the cave as a milk house.

We sat in its cool recess, and while gazing out on the silent scene and realising the past, one of us sang "Flora Macdonald's Lament," by the Ettrick Shepherd, a powerful poem, though untrue to fact. We also listened to another as he gave, in the native tongue, translating the sentiments for Saxon ears, "Welcome, Prince Charlie, to the land of Clanranald," by the soldier poet of the Rebellion, Alister Macdonald of Ardnamurchan. These songs, singularly appropriate to the scene, in description, allusion, and spirit, intensified our impressions.

As soon as possible after brave Clanranald's visit to Prince Charlie in the rude hovel on the eastern shore of Benbecula, where he had taken shelter at the close of his fruitless voyage to Stornoway, he was transferred to this more secure retreat. He was attended during his stay by some of his staunchest adherents, who would willingly have died for his sake, so ardently were they attached to him. In this cave and its neighbourhood, he remained nearly a month without his hiding-place being discovered by the enemy. It was known, however, to most of the natives, who, in talking of the Prince, used to call him "The Fair-haired Shepherd" and "The Yellow-haired Shepherd," in order not to betray him to the disaffected. Despite the enormous reward, they scorned to touch the price of blood; feeling, like old Kingsburgh, that "gold and silver piled heaps upon heaps to the bulk of yon huge mountain would not have tempted them for a moment to so foul, though profitable, a deed."

Charles did not spend his time entirely in painful hiding. From the security of his position, he was accustomed, like the crofters round him, to fish off the neighbouring shore, and even pursue the stag and shoot the game that abounded in the forest.

He was not left alone, for his friends held constant communication with him through trusty and wary messengers. By means of newspapers, secretly conveyed to him by Lady Margaret of Monkstadt, he was kept cognisant of the progress of events in hunting down his chivalrous followers and in searching for himself. At times, the remarkable safety of the place made him foolhardy in exposing himself, and he was not seldom in imminent danger of capture. Parties of soldiers who wandered everywhere, occasionally found their way near Glen Corrodale, and unknown to themselves, more than once actually saw the man they sought, who escaped only by his great presence of mind. His friends at Nunton. only a few miles distant, were unremitting in their kindly services.

CHAPTER VI.

THE HEROINE PREPARING FOR ACTION.

SOON the need of promptest measures for the Prince's escape from the Long Island became daily more urgent. The Government, feeling certain that he was concealed in Uist, sent more ships and troops under the fiercest and most vigilant of officers, to draw the toils closer round the audacious Pretender. Glen Corrodale or its neighbourhood now became suspected of holding the coveted prize. Fresh ships and soldiers arrived to extinguish the last ray of hope. Escape through such a cordon by land and sea looked impossible.

The rapidly increasing peril of his position was made known to the Prince by Boisdale, Clanranald's brother, who lived in the south end of South Uist, and by Balishare his kinsman, who dwelt in an island of that name, north of Benbecula. Balishare had been the kindly and faithful medium of communication between the Prince and Lady Margaret in Skye, who now sent the needed warning to his friends in Uist. Under untold risks, they paid him a secret visit, of which Balishare has left a plain but graphic account. They spent three days with him in happy disregard of surrounding terrors, if not in jovial merriment, a natural reaction against desperate conditions.

After they went, the Prince indulged the worst fears, and precipitately left his hiding place. He skirted the shore under night, first north to Benbecula, and then south to Loch Boisdale, landing vainly at different points in search of safety. All hope of promised assistance from his recent kindly visitors was blasted by the speedy apprehension of Boisdale. Charles now for a time became almost desperate. Dismissing all his attendants except Captain O'Neil, he fled northwards overland in the darkness. After strangely escaping capture, he returned to his old haunts on Hecla. Had help not arisen at this most critical juncture in his evil fortunes, the poor wanderer would certainly have fallen into the hands of his relentless foes, and the strange drama have issued in tragedy.

It was at this hour of direst need that he was rescued by our maiden of four-and-twenty summers. The manner in which this was done when hope seemed dead—in its self-possessed prosecution of a well-matured, daring plan—makes it quite remarkable as being the achievement of one so young and untried, an achievement almost as unique in its kind as that of Charlotte Corday.

It is simply extraordinary how the chief fugitive himself always escaped, often "by the skin of his teeth," while every one of his attendants, and Flora herself, fell rapidly into the net that enclosed the hunted band. The very tempests seemed favourable, and while saving time, bore him where he wished. When what seemed evil fortune caused a deviation from the plan at the landing place in Skye, that was the very turn that led to final success. Even the assistance of one of the very Government officers sent to seize the outlaw, without which escape was impossible, came, however improbably, at the moment it was needed. Such strange but fortunate experiences, combined with the many hairbreadth risks he successfully ran, were certainly sufficient to give the poor Prince the conviction he firmly gained, that he was himself, if not his enterprise, under the special protection of Heaven. Unfortunately, on the other hand, he barely missed speedy deliverance by means of a French cutter, sent for the purpose, which arrived in Uist three days after he had left, and which bore his late attendant, O'Sullivan, to France!

After much anxious consultation, details were finally fixed, to be carried out with all speed, for every hour's delay increased the danger. The Prince was to accompany Flora Macdonald to Skye, dressed as an Irish maid, called "Betty Burke," the name being evidently suggested by that of Ned

Burke, who was with the Prince in the Long Island and in Corrodale.

Flora could not leave Uist without dutifully acquainting her brother with the issues proposed, and seeing once more, and possibly for the last time, the dear home at Milton. Her tender sympathy and strength of purpose were severely tested by both the entreaties and hard words of her brother, whom she greatly loved, when she told him of the scheme. But, unmoved by his strong appeals to affection and interest, she remained inexorable in her courageous determination.

One evening when at Milton, a wanderer entered the house, whom she at once recognised as Captain O'Neil, having met him at Nunton. He had casually come to inquire regarding the movements of the military, and had left the Prince seated on a boulder not far from the door! The shrinking girl was then, for the first time, introduced to the fugitive; and the stone is still pointed out as the spot where the two chief actors in this drama first met. Fuller details of the proposed plans for rescue were there given by Flora—the generous O'Neil enthusiastically demonstrating to her, as he says, "the honour and immortality that would redound to her by such a glorious action," and Charles more quietly, but truly, expressing his sense of "so conspicuous a service."[1] The visitors departed for Corrodale.

On her return, the whole enterprise for a time seemed about to be wrecked, for she

---

[1] See Chambers. O'Neil claimed the honour of *first suggesting* the idea and the plan of the rescue, but these claims are contradicted by the dates and the facts; though, during their execution, he acted admirably, and suffered for it afterwards.

was made prisoner at the South Ford, which had to be crossed to reach Nunton, by the guard of soldiers placed there to arrest all wayfarers after dark. Through the happiest coincidence, they were under the command of her step-father, who was secretly friendly to the Prince. His early arrival next morning, for she was detained all night, dissipated Flora's fears. It not only secured her immediate release, but enabled her to obtain from him, without delay, the passport requisite for her plans; for no boat could leave the islands, under any pretence, without a permit from a responsible officer. The one she received allowed a passage to Skye for herself, a man-servant, and an Irish spinning-maid, with six of a crew. It was accompanied by an open letter to Captain Macdonald's wife, her own mother, recommending " Betty Burke " as a good spinster, and saying that she sent her daughter, "lest she should be in any way frightened with the troops lying here."

The needful equipment of the Prince was made by the kindly fingers of the Nunton ladies. It was skilfully chosen, as the Irish element allowed latitude of stride and ungainly feminine manners. The dress included a large gray Irish hood of dun camlet, which helped to conceal his tell-tale head and hair. The one thing, and that not the least important, which the ladies could not supply, was the proper management of his feet and skirts. Forgetfulness of these feminine punctilios went far to mar the plot in Skye.[1]

[1] A bit of the gown, a flowered cotton, and part of the string that tied the white apron, are still preserved in the third volume of the M.S. copy of the "Lyon in Mourning," by Bishop Forbes, in eight priceless volumes, presented by Robert Chambers to the Advocates' Library, where these relics are shown to visitors.

CHAPTER VII.

THE HEROINE IN ACTION.

THE Prince and O'Neil left Corrodale by boat, and landed at Rossnish in Benbecula, where first he had come after Culloden. O'Neil left him in the old and now familiar hovel, and stealthily crossed the watery moors to Nunton, to complete requisite measures with his friends.

On the 26th of June, Flora and Lady Clanranald, accompanied by Neil MacEachan, were guided by O'Neil through the dangerous bogs and lakes, to the hiding-place of the fugitive. The spot was not far from the shore, to favour escape, and in sight of the very vessels scouring the Minch for him. They found royalty in miserable garb, cooking part of a captured sheep, a sight that drew female tears. He received his visitors with the brightest affability and all the courtly manners of France. At his invitation, they seated themselves at his board, a stone laid on a pillar of turf, to partake of his mess. To this were added some dainties kindly brought by the ladies from the mansion. Their distinguished host did the honours of the table with surprising humour and perfect grace. Where could a more picturesque or singular subject be found for painter or poet than such a scene, on Prince Charlie's last night in the Long Island!

After the repast, the Prince retired with O'Neil behind a peat hagg, to dress for the tragic play, and soon presented himself to the expectant ladies as "Betty." Her appearance and behaviour, after some further adjustment, were pronounced satisfactory, and increased the hopes of freedom.

Just then the sudden noise of coming feet struck terror into every heart. It turned out to be a breathless messenger from Nunton, quickly followed by a second, urging Lady Clanranald's immediate return, as two Government officers, one of them Captain Ferguson, the most violent of them all, had just arrived there on well-founded suspicion. She set out at once, guided through the wild mosses by the gillies, and it was only through skilful fence that she was able to hide her difficult errand. Flora remained for some time in the hut, to lessen the gathering danger, and to explain her plans in greater detail. These were entered into keenly, if not merrily, by the petticoated Prince; but

Flora firmly refused the ardent entreaties of the devoted O'Neil to accompany them to Skye, as hazarding success.

The toils were closing sternly round the poor hunted stag, for O'Neil was speedily apprehended at the South Ford. It was now or never for the hope of the Jacobites! Yet, as not seldom at other critical moments of fate, the burden of destiny rested on what seemed the weakest shoulders—here those of a quiet girl of twenty-four.

That evening, when O'Neil and MacEachan conducted Flora to Nunton, to spend the last night with her friends, before next day facing the danger and death that have immortalised her name, the poor Prince was left in absolute loneliness.

How intense and how various both thought and feeling in his breast during the long, long silent hours of that summer night, in that miserable refuge amid the mosses of Benbecula! Not even the anniversary of Culloden at Versailles, so well sung by Aytoun, could have stirred deeper emotion; for the past was troubled, the present hazardous, and the future dark. What must have been his throbs of astonished gratitude as he thought of the extraordinary devotion of the woman whose return he waited on the morrow! How slowly must have lagged the weary hours of the next day, while he peered from the hut to watch the passing sails that bore relentless foes, and scarcely dared to venture forth for fear of betraying all!

Late that night, the 27th of June, Flora and MacEachan joined the anxious man, already attired for the perilous voyage, and nervously impatient to realise his fate. At ten, in a drenching rain, the three set out in silent circumspection for the shore, where Clanranald's boat had been appointed to meet them. There they kindled a dangerous but needed fire, while awaiting its arrival, which, from unforeseen causes, was painfully delayed. To their horror, as the smoke rose heavily heavenwards, they caught sight of several wherries bearing redcoats, which seemed making for the very point where they camped! Instantly stamping out the traitor flame, they crouched in the dripping heather, breathless with apprehension. But this last hazard at length disappeared in the darkness, and left them in unspeakable relief. At midnight, the well-appointed boat, manned by six stalwart, selected clansmen, touched the shore and bore them out into the welcome deep. Nigh forty miles of open sea stretched black before them, under gathering clouds; but hope pointed the way, and courage plied the oar.

Soon the furious storm, with thunder and lightning, descended upon them, and drove them helplessly before it. Happily, it bore them towards Scotland, and shortened their voyage. Peace came with the early dawn, which but revealed the waste of waters. To cheer his weary friends, the good Prince sang a bright old song about the Restoration of his ancestors, and told some pleasant stories. Gradually the peaks of the Coolins pierced the waning gloom, and they made for the nearest shore, the coast of Waternish.

To their dismay, they were greeted with bullets from a party of soldiers stationed there, but no one was wounded, though the rudder handle was snapped. While the fusillade lasted, the Prince urged Flora to crouch for safety in the bottom of the boat.

This she refused to do till he did the same, saying that his life was more precious than hers. The boat at the soldiers' command was luckily without oars, and they escaped unscathed.

Exhausted and sleepless, they coasted slowly along the bold, volcanic cliffs of Skye, while Flora slumbered on the ballast, in the reaction after the fateful days and troublous night, tenderly watched by her royal companion.

They landed at last, on that Saturday afternoon, near Monkstadt, the residence of Flora's friend and the Prince's well-wisher, Lady Margaret. She had sent him newspapers to the cave at Corrodale, as already told; and she had lately taken unsuccessful measures for his rescue, and received a letter of thanks from the royal hand—a relic which, to her lasting regret, safety required to be destroyed. Charles sprang elated to the beach, as if at last clutching freedom in his eager grasp, though nearly three more months of weary and terrible wandering passed before he found it.

CHAPTER VIII.

THE HEROINE COMPLETING HER WORK.

MONKSTADT stands on an eminence overlooking St. Columba's Loch, then large and beautiful, and not far from the western flanks of the Quiraing. Beyond the loch are the church and graveyard of Kilmuir, in the greenest part of the island; and the beautiful country round, long known as "the granary of Skye," was inhabited by industrious and contented crofters.

The Prince took shelter in a small cave, now gone, to which Flora's baggage had been removed. After refreshment, which excitement had made them forget till then, the boatmen returned to Uist, visible across the Minch. This early departure was the one mistake in the whole conduct of the rescue; for the boat was at once seized on landing, the boatmen were cross-examined, and only a day or two after his prey had escaped, fierce Ferguson arrived in Skye, and caused the immediate apprehension of those concerned.

Fortunately, Sir Alexander Macdonald was then at Fort Augustus, in attendance on Cumberland; but his wife was at home, where also Kingsburgh, the good old factor, had arrived, urged, he said, by a strange impulse. Among the visitors was a certain Captain Macleod, a rude officer, in command of a detachment of militia stationed at Uig, not far off, whose presence, while a real source of danger, only evoked the brave adroitness of the ladies.

Though at once ushered into the drawing-room among the guests, with the redcoats there, Flora betrayed nothing, by either look or manner. After warm welcome from Lady Margaret, she was rigorously questioned by Macleod; and she not only disarmed his suspicions but won his devoted attentions. It was not till after dinner, to which the Captain escorted her, that she was able to break the news, to the judicious factor, of the trying watch of the Prince all these hours by the lonely shore. Though at first hysterical at the extreme hazard, on learning the facts, Lady Margaret quickly regained her usual tact and vivacity.

Kingsburgh and MacEachan soon joined the waiting fugitive with needed food and protection. Charles spent the night alone in the cave. After the dangerous officers had retired, a midnight consultation was held between the ladies, the factor, and a fine fellow, Captain Donald Roy Macdonald, honourably wounded at Culloden, who had been secretly summoned to assist. Plans were settled, and Roy rode off at once for Portree, to prepare the way there.

By daybreak next morning, the factor and the Prince set out; good Lady Margaret, who with Flora was astir, wisely restraining her longing to see the man for whom she risked so much. Later, Flora and another lady who was going to Portree followed on ponies, attended by MacEachan, after gay farewell to the baffled Macleod. Flora passed the Prince and his companion unheeded, and soon parting with her friend, who noted "the rude woman" walking with Kingsburgh, she returned to the pair.

They moved slowly on, sheltering themselves at times from drenching rain and fording the swollen streams, where the Prince's petticoats were both troublesome and dangerous. After leaving the pretty bay of Uig, they met the country folks coming from Snizort church, who talked with the affable factor, expressing amused surprise at "the rough, long-legged slattern" striding so sturdily along.

Late that night, they arrived at Kingsburgh house, which stood on Loch Snizort, not far from the shore. Mrs. Macdonald, who had retired, was soon introduced to Prince Charles, whose unfeminine style had at first frightened herself and her little daughter. At the bright supper, quickly prepared by the ladies, the petticoated prince sat on the right and Flora on the left of the motherly hostess. Then followed a genial hour or two, spent alone by the two men, amid the smoke of the Prince's old pipe and the steam of Kingsburgh's bowl—the happiest night, beyond dispute, Charles ever spent after Culloden. The scene, delightful in its natural details, was ended only by the gentle coercion of the old man to get his charmed guest to retire to rest. This was at last gained when the punch bowl broke in two in the jovial struggle, to be preserved as a memorial.

Next day, the weary wayfarer rose from bed, the first he had pressed for many a day, only when roused past noon. The two good women each folded up a sheet he had lain in, to be preserved for their burial, and Kingsburgh secured his worn brogues as a memento of the time. Breakfast past, the Prince was attired in "Betty's" garb, amidst the merriment of all. After hearty thanks to his hostess, who gave him her snuff-box as a keepsake, Charles set out with the factor, Flora, and MacEachan. On the way, the irksome costume was soon exchanged for a Highland suit of Kingsburgh's, and the two men parted with mutual emotion.

The Prince and his friends passed, by unfrequented paths, through scenery whose quiet beauty, with bright glimpses of the Coolins, doubtless soothed their anxious but hopeful hearts. In a rainy evening, they reached the rude hamlet of Portree, the King's Port, so named from Charles's ancestor, James V., who had visited it two hundred years before. They were received by Captain Roy and the young laird of Raasay, and conducted to the inn. Its publicity being hazardous, not least through the Prince's distinguished manners, his friends proposed retiring to the securer shelter of the cave on the northern shore of the bay, since then associated for ever with his name.

Now came the final separation between Prince Charlie and his fair preserver, in a heavy rain, which fell as if in sympathetic sadness. The parting was affecting and human. With gathering tears, he pressed her hands, thanked her fervently for all she had risked for him, presented her with a locket holding his miniature, and tenderly kissed her brow, hoping he would meet her again at the court of St. James. Then he disappeared for ever from her gaze, if not to forget her during the next forty-two years, at least to make no sign. They separated on the last day of June, 1746—he to die bankrupt in fortune and character, a broken old man of sixty-eight; she to become the heroine of the century, and a cherished name for all time.

Thus ended the extraordinary history of three short days. But how pregnant with fate! The popular poetry and painting that have glorified them, from Hogg to Aytoun, are almost without exception based on error, and celebrate scenes that never occurred. Never did "the bonnie young Flora sit sighing her lane;" never "in the wilds of far Kintail," or anything else, " did the cavern give them shelter;" never was hers the heart to ask, " Why slept the red bolt in the breast of the cloud?" Are not the simple facts unspeakably greater than the fairest fictions of the pen or the pencil?

CHAPTER IX.

THE HEROINE IN STATE CAPTIVITY.

DONALD ROY returned to Kingsburgh and Monkstadt to tell his friends the issue. The hunted wanderer remained in the cave with the young laird and others till near daylight, when they crossed to Raasay, the island just opposite Portree. They hid there in a hovel, but came back afterwards to the Quiraing, seeking safety. With a single trusty henchman, Charles then walked right through the most unfrequented tracts to near Broadford, and at last reached the Mainland on lonely Loch Nevis, on the fifth day since parting with

Flora. Then followed wanderings, wide, wild and wonderful, by land and sea, lake and mountain top, from Loch Morar in Arisaig to Loch Monar in Ross—the Prince sometimes passing between sentinels within gun-shot, and often narrowly escaping capture and death. From the very spot where he first landed at Borrodale, he set sail for France, on the 20th of September, five months after the fatal day on Drummossie Moor, and more than forty years before his death, on the 30th of January, 1788, two years before that of his fair deliverer.

The captive was free. But his brave liberators had now to face the durance or death from which they had rescued him. The Government, under the pitiless counsels of a Cumberland, were in no mood to be trifled with, especially in dealing with those who had dared to snatch the prey from their very grasp. At once, the incredible tale of the Prince's escape from Uist electrified the nation and enraged the Court. Swift measures were taken to secure the felons. Several eluded pursuit, but most of them were imprisoned; Clanranald and his lady in the Tower, and aged Kingsburgh, first in Fort Augustus, and afterwards in Edinburgh Castle.

After leaving Portree, Flora visited her mother at Armadale in Sleat, in the south of Skye. To save her feelings, with unexampled and beautiful firmness and reserve, Flora told her nothing of her connection with the prince! She returned to Uist, after a few days, to meet her friends and relieve their anxiety. From Milton, however, she was speedily summoned back to Skye, to answer the gravest charges. Indignantly repelling all friendly counsels to hide in the wilds of Hecla till the storm should subside, she surrendered herself unattended. She freely confessed the whole, declaring it a service for which she never could repent or express a moment's regret. She was arrested and conveyed on board a war vessel, in which she again met the captive O'Neil. Kind General Campbell allowed her to land at Armadale, to take farewell of her mother and prepare for her long journey. Attended by a simple Highland girl, who knew only Gaelic and who remained with her in London, she was carried first to Dunstaffnage Castle and then to Leith Roads.

There she remained for weeks, confined to the troopship, but kindly treated and visited by enthusiastic hundreds. Amidst all the excitement, says good Bishop Forbes of Leith, who often met her, "her wise conduct in one of the most perplexing scenes that can happen in life, her fortitude and good sense, are memorable instances of the strength of a female mind, even in those years that are tender and inexperienced."

On the 7th November, amidst a great ovation, she set sail for London. There she was at first committed to the Tower. But popular feeling in favour of "the Prince's Preserver," as she was called, was much too strong to permit of any punishment, and she spent a year in the capital among titled friends, as a prisoner on parole. Admiration of her dauntless deed knew no bounds, and the time passed in a succession of receptions of all ranks, as by the queen of hearts. Even royalty itself came to tender its homage to this charming rebel; and highborn dames expressed themselves "willing to wipe her shoes." Enthusiasm was increased by the inexplicable simplicity, modest self-possession, and calm good sense exhibited by one so young, under the incense of flattery which would have intoxicated all but the wisest, or, as Chambers puts it, "would have turned the heads of ninety-nine of a hundred women of any age, country, or condition." Fashion was still more astonished at the accomplished manners, the courtly ease and grace, and the entire absence of provincial rusticity and Highland accent, in a girl from the western wilds—for, as Bishop Forbes naively remarks, "No lady, Edinburgh bred, could acquit herself better at the tea-table!"

Flora Macdonald was no common-place heroine, conscious, attitudinising, and melodramatic. This only increased the perplexity she created, and intensified universal regard. To all that met her, she was a phenomenon from the savage north, an edelweiss[1] that had bloomed on the edge of a glacier. And a true edelweiss she was—a beautiful example of nobleness and purity! There was very much more in her character than the "courage and fidelity" of Johnson's panegyric. The more it is studied, the more does admiration rise of its rare simplicity, real ability, and high-toned goodness.

[1] The beautiful flower that blooms on the snows of the Alps; its name being derived from the German *edel*, noble (represented in the name Ethel), and *weiss*, white.

CHAPTER X.

THE HEROINE IN AFTER LIFE.

THE after history of Flora Macdonald only raises the esteem her early goodness and courage inspire.

When pardoned in 1847, she could not rest till she had gained freedom for all her captive friends. For dear Kingsburgh, she was specially solicitous. This fine old Highland gentleman had been treated with cruel severity; he being put in irons at Fort Augustus, and even his death being contemplated by bloody Cumberland.

Loaded with costly presents and a liberal dowry, Flora left London in a coach and four, with her Highland maid and faithful Neil MacEachan, whose high spirits blossomed into Gaelic song, in celebration of the "wisdom and courage" of his mistress. After bright reception in Edinburgh and Inverness, she rode all the way to Armadale to see her mother. Thence she made a succession of visits to her Skye friends, welcomed everywhere with enthusiastic pride, and not least so at Kingsburgh. At Monkstadt, a splendid banquet was prepared in her honour, to which the chief people in Skye and the Islands were invited, including the Clanranalds from Nunton and her good brother from Milton.

From the giddy elevation she had attained, she then retired unobtrusively and of natural choice to the calm, secluded life she had but temporarily, though brilliantly, left. Along with her brother, she went back to the dear cottage by the mill on the quiet Loch of Kildonan. There she spent two years, keeping her brother's house and living among her people and her friends,—at once the greatest heroine of the age and the simplest of women.

Though she might have wedded riches and rank, which would have been proud to have added such a jewel to the oldest coronet, she chose rather to be united to the lowly Highland lad who had won her heart at Monkstadt, poor but handsome Allan Macdonald, Kingsburgh's son. In November, 1750, in her twenty-ninth year, they married, and began the old plain life of a farm, which Flora loved so well, at Floddigarry in the north of Skye.

Floddigarry occupies one of the most romantic positions in Skye, not far from Loch Staffin, amid grassy knolls, under the frowning magnificence of the Quiraing, with a splendid outlook to the mountainous Mainland across the sea. For more than twenty years, she lived there in happy retirement, surrounded by friends and tenants, Lady Margaret's mansion being but a few miles distant, and devoted to a growing handsome family, which ultimately numbered nine. In 1772, on the death of the good factor, they removed to fair Kingsburgh—a comfortable thatched house, like her brother's at Milton, —now only represented by a few plane trees that grew round the garden.

There, in 1773, she charmed Dr. Samuel Johnson during his unique Highland journey. He found her, then above fifty, "a woman of soft features, gentle manners and elegant presence." Boswell describes her as "of genteel appearance, and uncommonly mild and well-bred;" and her husband as being "completely the figure of a gallant Highlander, exhibiting the graceful mien and manly looks which our popular Scotch song has justly attributed to that character."

Then came straitened circumstances, shared at that period by many others in Skye, who emigrated to America to improve their condition. Thither also followed Allan Macdonald and his family, in 1774, to Carolina, where a flourishing Highland settlement had risen. There Flora was warmly welcomed with festivities held in her honour.

Now fell the first family sorrow, in the death of her two youngest children, whose graves are still preserved in that distant land, in memory of their mother.

At that time, the American war burst out. Allan Macdonald became brigadier-general in 1776, and his five gallant sons officers in the royal forces and one in the navy. In spite of entreaty, Flora at first shared with her husband all the hardships of the campaign, impelled by the brave and affectionate heart she always bore. He was, however, unfortunately captured and imprisoned by the successful colonists. In 1779, at his request, Flora returned to Britain, along with her younger daughter, after five years' absence. On the voyage, the undying courage of youth was once more exhibited. The ship being attacked by a French privateer, she remained on deck during the fight, inspiring the men, and had her arm broken.

Strangely, but appropriately, she sojourned for a time in the spot to which her thoughts ever turned, dear unforgotten Milton. There her brother built her a house, not far from her birthplace, on Loch

Kildonan, opposite the ancient graveyard, where its ruins are still visible; and to this quiet home, brave Allan came on his release, as Captain on half pay.

They settled down ere long for the rest of their days, at old Kingsburgh, with its pleasant scenery and its pregnant memories. Her daughters both married well, and her sons attained distinction in the army and navy; the eldest being characterised by Lord Macdonald at his grave, as "the most finished gentleman of his family and name."

In serene age, our heroine calmly died, close on seventy years old, attended by her devoted husband and daughters, on the 5th of March, 1790. She was wrapped in the sheet, in which had strangely slept both the Stewart prince and the English moralist, and which, unlike one so young, she had chosen for her shroud nearly fifty years before. She received an honoured burial in the churchyard of Kilmuir, near the spot where she had brought the Prince to Skye, and midway between Kingsburgh and Floddigarry, where she had spent so many happy days.

The marble slab first placed on her grave by one of her sons, Colonel Macdonald, was chipped to pieces and carried off as mementoes by enthusiastic visitors, as from the shrine of a saint.

An obelisk, erected by admirers, now marks the place where reposes the dust of one who had proved herself, beyond dispute, " A woman nobly planned."

"Give me back my trusty comrades!
　　Give me back my Highland maid!
　Nowhere beats the heart so kindly
　　As beneath the tartan plaid!"

Aytoun.

www.ingramcontent.com/pod-product-compliance
Lightning Source LLC
Chambersburg PA
CBHW032244080426
42735CB00008B/992